SHORT WALKS
ISLE OF WIGHT

by Paul Curtis

Causeway through Bembridge Harbour (Walk 1)

CONTENTS

Using this guide... 4
Route summary table 6
Map key 7
Introduction.. 9
  Walking on the Isle of Wight....................................... 9
  Where to stay.. 10
  Getting there and around... 11

The walks
  1. St Helens village and shoreline 13
  2. Brading and Nunwell Down.................................. 17
  3. Sandown and Shanklin 23
  4. Newchurch and the River Yar 29
  5. Godshill and Freemantle Gate 33
  6. Ventnor and Bonchurch...................................... 39
  7. Niton Undercliff and St Catherine's Lighthouse..... 43
  8. St Catherine's Down... 49
  9. Afton Down and Compton Down 53
  10. Freshwater to Alum Bay..................................... 59
  11. Alum Bay to Colwell 65
  12. Yarmouth and the Western Yar estuary 71
  13. Newtown and Newtown Harbour 75
  14. Newport and Carisbrooke................................... 81
  15. Ryde to Fishbourne.. 87

Useful information.. 94

USING THIS GUIDE

Routes in this book

In this book you will find a selection of easy or moderate walks suitable for almost everyone, including casual walkers and families with children, or for when you only have a short time to fill. The routes have been carefully chosen to allow you to explore the area and its attractions. Most routes are circular, although some linear walks are included that use public transport to get back to the start. Although there may be some climbs there is no challenging terrain, but do bear in mind that conditions can sometimes be wet or muddy underfoot. A route summary table is included on page 6 to help you choose the right walk.

Clothing and footwear

You won't need any special equipment to enjoy these walks. The weather in Britain can be changeable, so choose clothing suitable for the season and wear or carry a waterproof jacket. For footwear, comfortable walking boots or trainers with a good grip are best. A small rucksack for drinks, snacks and spare clothing is useful. See www.adventuresmart.uk.

Walk descriptions

At the beginning of each walk you'll find all the information you need:

- start/finish location, with a what3words address to help you find it
- parking and transport information, estimated walking time, total distance and climb
- details of public toilets available along the route and where you can get refreshments
- a summary of the key highlights of the walk and what you might see

Timings given are the time to complete the walk at a reasonable walking pace. Allow extra time for extended stops or if walking with children.

The route is described in clear, easy-to-follow directions, with each waypoint marked on an accompanying map extract. It's a good idea to read the whole of the route instructions before setting out, so that you know what to expect.

Maps, GPX files and what3words

Extracts from the OS® 1:25,000 map accompany each route. GPX files for all the walks in this book are available to download at www.cicerone.co.uk/1255/gpx.

What3words is a free smartphone app which identifies every 3m square of the globe with a unique three-word address, e.g. ///destiny.cafe.sonic. For more information see https://what3words.com/products/what3words-app.

USING THIS GUIDE

Walking with children

Even young children can be surprisingly strong walkers, but every family is different and you may need to adapt the timings given in this book to take that into account. Make sure you go at the pace of the slowest member and choose a walk with an exciting objective in mind, such as a cave, river, waterfall or picnic spot. Many of the walks can be shortened to suit – suggestions are included at the end of the route description.

Dogs

Sheep or cattle may be found grazing on a number of these walks. Keep dogs under control at all times so that they don't scare or disturb livestock or wildlife. Cattle, particularly cows with calves, may very occasionally pose a risk to walkers with dogs. If you ever feel threatened by cattle, you should let go of your dog's lead and let it run free.

Enjoying the countryside responsibly

Enjoy the countryside and treat it with respect to protect our natural environments. Stick to footpaths and take your litter home with you. When driving, slow down on rural roads and park considerately, or better still use public transport. For more details check out www.gov.uk/countryside-code.

The Countryside Code

Respect everyone
- be considerate to those living in, working in and enjoying the countryside
- leave gates and property as you find them
- do not block access to gateways or driveways when parking
- be nice, say hello, share the space
- follow local signs and keep to marked paths unless wider access is available

Protect the environment
- take your litter home – leave no trace of your visit
- do not light fires and only have BBQs where signs say you can
- always keep dogs under control and in sight
- dog poo – bag it and bin it – any public waste bin will do
- care for nature – do not cause damage or disturbance

Enjoy the outdoors
- check your route and local conditions
- plan your adventure – know what to expect and what you can do
- enjoy your visit, have fun, make a memory

ROUTE SUMMARY TABLE

WALK NAME	START POINT	TIME	DISTANCE
1. St Helens village and shoreline	The Vine Inn, St Helens	1hr 15min	4.6km (2.9 miles)
2. Brading and Nunwell Down	Brading station	1hr 30min	5.1km (3.2 miles)
3. Sandown and Shanklin	Sandown Pier	1hr 45min	7km (4.3 miles)
4. Newchurch and the River Yar	The Pointer Inn, Newchurch	1hr 15min	4.1km (2.5 miles)
5. Godshill and Freemantle Gate	The Griffin pub, Godshill	1hr 30min	5.2km (3.2 miles)
6. Ventnor and Bonchurch	Ventnor seafront	1hr	4.1km (2.5 miles)
7. Niton Undercliff and St Catherine's Lighthouse	Niton church	1hr 45min	6.8km (4.2 miles)
8. St Catherine's Down	Blackgang Viewpoint car park	1hr 15min	4.6km (2.9 miles)
9. Afton Down and Compton Down	Freshwater Bay	2hr 30min	10km (6.2 miles)
10. Freshwater to Alum Bay	Stroud Recreation Ground, Freshwater	2hr 15min	8.6km (5.3 miles)
11. Alum Bay to Colwell	Needles Landmark Attraction, Alum Bay	1hr 15min	4.4km (2.7 miles)
12. Yarmouth and the Western Yar estuary	Yarmouth bus station/ ferry terminal	1hr 45min	6.7km (4.2 miles)
13. Newtown and Newtown Harbour	Newtown National Trust visitor centre	40min	2.4km (1.5 miles)
14. Newport and Carisbrooke	Newport bus station	1hr 30min	5.7km (3.5 miles)
15. Ryde to Fishbourne	Ryde Esplanade station	1hr 30min	5.4km (3.4 miles)

ROUTE SUMMARY TABLE

HIGHLIGHTS
Causeway across harbour, beach, St Helen's Old Church
Views from Brading Down, butterfly walk, Roman villa
Protected clifftop walking and promenade linking two resorts
Newchurch Moors Nature Reserve, Yar River Trail
Godshill church, views, woodland, Freemantle Gate
Sea wall, Old Church and long pond at Bonchurch
Magnificent sea views, beautiful Undercliff, Victorian lighthouse
Coastal views, Hoy Monument, medieval lighthouse
All about the sea views!
Thrilling seascapes, Tennyson Monument, the Needles
Headon Warren, stunning views, lovely sea wall
Easy walking beside river estuary, Freshwater Old Village
Peaceful village with fascinating history, nature reserve
The island's capital, Carisbrooke Castle
Abbey ruins, magnificent Quarr Abbey and tea garden

SYMBOLS USED ON ROUTE MAPS

(S) Start point

(F) Finish point

(SF) Start and finish at the same place

 Waypoint

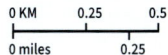 Route line

MAPPING IS SHOWN AT A SCALE OF 1:25,000

```
0 KM      0.25      0.5
0 miles         0.25
```

DOWNLOAD THE GPX FILES FOR FREE AT
www.cicerone.co.uk/1255/gpx

Footpath junction near Godshill (Walk 5)

INTRODUCTION

The island has a convoluted topography

The Isle of Wight is only a short ferry ride away from the south coast but feels more cut off from the rest of mainland Britain than it actually is. Nearly half the island has been designated a National Landscape, and as well as the great variety of landscape visitors will find unique towns, villages and resorts, each of which has its own character. There are around 525km of footpaths; the topography of the island means that many of these are very steep, but this book purposely ignores them, choosing easier but just as beautiful routes, showing the very best of the island.

Walking on the Isle of Wight

The 15 walks in this book incorporate all areas of the island from Newtown Harbour in the north, Niton Undercliff in the south, St Helens and Brading in the east, and the chalk cliffs of High Down (near the Needles) in the west. Most of the walks are circular, and for the three that are not, a short bus ride returns you to the start. The walks are not entirely flat, but where there are hills, these are never too strenuous and never too long. If you have had enough of walking, do allow time to visit Osborne House (Queen Victoria's

Ventnor seafront (Walk 6)

favourite home) and also Carisbrooke Castle.

Most walks feature dramatic sea views as a matter of course and a few follow the island's famed Coastal Path. These sea views are often best appreciated from the island's many areas of downland, such as St Catherine's Down in the south (Walk 8), and High Down near the Needles (Walk 10). There are other charms, such as the lovely walk around Newtown Harbour Nature Reserve (Walk 13), the pretty inland ramble through the woodland around Newchurch (Walk 4), visiting sandy beaches at Ryde or Totland Bay (Walk 11), or even attractive footpaths linking Newport and Carisbrooke Castle (Walk 14).

Where to stay

Most visitors stay in one of the seaside resorts on the east of the island: Sandown, Shanklin or Ventnor. There are numerous hotels and B&Bs to suit all budgets in all three places. Sandown generally offers the lowest rates and Ventnor the highest, with prices varying according to season but 'mini-peaking' over Christmas and New Year.

While the resorts certainly make excellent choices for a walking break, there are less conventional alternatives. Interesting and often upmarket places can be found in areas such as Seaview and Niton Undercliff; and private rooms through websites such as Airbnb (Airbnb.co.uk), camping and other self-catering options can be found all over the island, sometimes in

Freshwater Bay (Walks 9 and 10)

pleasingly remote locations. Newport has budget chain hotels as well as a few boutique hotels and makes a good base for travellers relying on public transport who wish to visit the whole island and prefer the bustle of a town. Ryde and Cowes also offer a sprinkling of registered accommodation. There is a YHA hostel in Totland (www.yha.org.uk).

Ryde Pier (Walk 15)

Getting there and around

The only way to get to the Isle of Wight is by sea, with ferries from Portsmouth to Ryde, from Southampton to East and West Cowes, and from Lymington to Yarmouth respectively (for more details see 'Useful information' on page 94). Services vary in frequency but are all typically hourly; timetables can be found online. Tickets for car and foot passengers can be bought both in advance and at the port, and there are usually discounts for regular travellers, so check the operators' websites before purchasing. Through-train/ferry tickets can be bought to any train station on the Island Line (which runs between Ryde Pier and Shanklin), as well as to Cowes, East Cowes and Yarmouth.

Taking a car onto the ferry can be expensive, so it might be wiser to leave your vehicle on the mainland. The island's bus service, operated by Southern Vectis, is excellent: comprehensive and usually extremely reliable. All the walks in this book are accessible by bus apart from Walks 4 and 13, and a bus journey across the island from Ryde or Sandown to Alum Bay takes about 90min. A user-friendly bus timetable is available at Newport, Yarmouth and Ryde bus stations and from the Southern Vectis website (www.islandbuses.info).

In season, special hop-on-hop-off buses catering for tourists complement the usual routes, but premium fares are charged. There is also a seasonal Island Coaster service running clockwise from Ryde to Yarmouth every morning and returning from Alum Bay every afternoon (two or three services daily). This can be especially handy for travelling to the 'Back of the Wight'.

The island's road network is good and traffic jams are unusual aside from a few hotspots. Parking is often free or low cost, and details are provided for each walk.

St Helen's Old Church

WALK 1
St Helens village and shoreline

Start/finish	*The Vine Inn, St Helens*
Locate	*///attaching.airtime.desk*
Cafes/pubs	*Pub and cafes in St Helens Green, cafe and restaurant at seafront*
Transport	*Bus route 8*
Parking	*St Helens Green car park (PO33 1UJ)*
Toilets	*On St Helens Green (year round) and beside the seafront cafe (seasonal)*

Time 1hr 15min
Distance 4.6km (2.9 miles)
Climb 50m

A bit of everything on this easy walk: a village green, a long causeway, a beach, and a ruined church by the water's edge

Many places on the island have their own special ambience and St Helens is one of them. After soaking in the atmosphere of the village green, saunter down to Bembridge Harbour where a causeway leads to 'the Duver' and a popular family-orientated beach. Here is all that remains of St Helen's Old Church, its one remaining side used these days as a seamark to aid navigation at sea. Pretty field paths and other footpaths return you to the Vine Inn.

Boats on Bembridge Harbour

SHORT WALKS ISLE OF WIGHT

The Vine Inn in St Helens

1 From the Vine Inn, cross the road and bear half-left across the village green to locate and descend quiet Mill Road. At the end of the road (which is actually more of a footpath), turn left beside Bembridge Harbour to follow the **Coastal Path**.

2 The sea wall becomes a delightful **causeway** through the harbour. This leads to the Duver, an island word meaning sand dunes. At the end of the causeway turn sharp right on a stony path. Soon pass near a water activity centre and keep on towards the colourful beach huts visible ahead. Turn left to walk past the huts along the short promenade which culminates at the tower of **St Helen's Old Church**, with attractive beaches on both sides.

> The tower is all that remains of a 13th-century church that started disintegrating in Tudor times and fell out of use. In 1703 it was

The causeway through the harbour

WALK 1 – ST HELENS VILLAGE AND SHORELINE

bricked up, and some years later was replaced by a new church further inland.

3 At the church stay on the tarmac and in 100m turn right through a gate, following the Coastal Path sign. Continue through two fields, linked by a footbridge over a stream (it doesn't matter which fork you take just after it). Ascend the second field and exit its far-right corner, then turn right into a lane and soon bear left into the drive of the **Priory Bay Hotel**.

4 In 250m a footpath branches away from the drive and, at a path T-junction in 350m, turn left on footpath R83 to continue along the left-hand side of a field. Cross **Eddington Road** to the right and continue on footpath R82. Ignore a right fork in 550m, cross a residential road, and emerge back beside the Vine Inn.

St Helens Beach and Old Church

– To shorten
At St Helen's Old Church go straight up the lane to return directly to the village green (saves 20min or 1.4km).

St Helens

St Helens village green

The Saxon village was originally centred on the Duver. Then in the 1080s a Benedictine Priory, dedicated to St Helena, was established approximately where today's Priory Bay Hotel stands. A French invasion was repelled in 1340, and six years later it was from here that Edward III left to successfully invade Normandy. Nelson too departed from St Helens, for the Battle of Trafalgar, and it is said that the village was his last view of England. The village green is a conservation area – the cottages are mainly 18th century and very few properties have been built since World War 2.

WALK 2
Brading and Nunwell Down

Time 1hr 30min
Distance 5.1km (3.2 miles)
Climb 115m

Start/finish	*Brading station*
Locate	*///sprains.flown.played*
Cafes/pubs	*Cafe at Brading Roman Villa*
Transport	*Train to Brading. Bus routes 2 and 3*
Parking	*Brading station car park (PO36 0DY)*
Toilets	*No public toilets on route (except inside Brading Roman Villa)*

A leafy track across Nunwell Down leads up onto a ridge with outstanding views, followed by a short butterfly walk and a Roman villa

Despite its shortness this is a very varied walk. The broad track from historic Brading across the face of Nunwell Down is lovely when the trees are in leaf. You are quite high already but ascend still further on a moderately steep path to the top of the down for wonderful views across Sandown Bay. Take in a pretty butterfly walk while descending Brading Down and return to Brading past its Roman villa (entrance fee).

View towards Brading from Nunwell Down

1 At the Sandown end of Platform 1, go through a metal gate to start the walk. Once at the main road (**A3055**), cross it and continue on Wrax Road opposite. Stay on this broad gravel road as it twists and turns to meet another tarmac road at Linden Terrace. Until the 16th century, Brading was a working port. After much of the harbour was drained in 1878, the town became less prosperous.

2 Cross the road to continue on bridleway B39. A short way along look through a gap in the bushes on your right for a great view of Brading below you. Ignore ways off the main track as it crosses the face of **Nunwell Down**, first ascending then descending and finally undulating. Having walked along the track for 1.2km bear sharp left uphill, following a blue arrow. If you look to your left while ascending you might get a glimpse of **Nunwell**

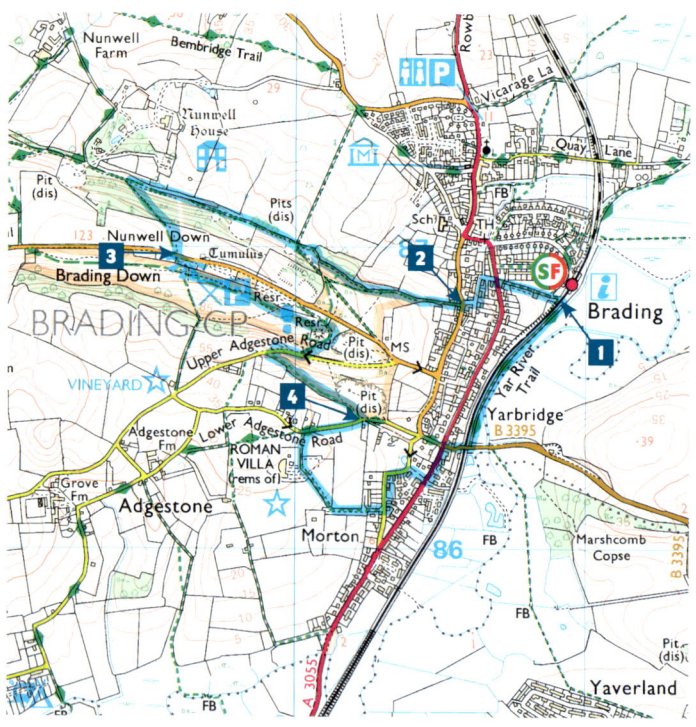

WALK 2 – BRADING AND NUNWELL DOWN

Track along Nunwell Down

House set in beautiful gardens. King Charles I spent his last night of freedom here before being imprisoned in Carisbrooke Castle. The woodland soon ends and you carry on over the grass to reach the Downs Road.

3 Cross the road from north-facing Nunwell Down onto south-facing **Brading Down** with an unbeatable view over Sandown Bay. Turn left, go through the wooden gate by a signpost, and continue along the ridge. Go through another gate in 450m, then at a path T-junction shortly beyond it turn right onto B41. Turn right on reaching **Upper Adgestone Road**, and immediately on your right start the 'Butterfly Walk'. This small reserve was created specifically to encourage butterflies, so nectar-producing flowers like the horseshoe vetch can be seen surrounding the short footpath. Soon

> ⓘ *Nearby Adgestone Vineyard is claimed to be the oldest continuously operated vineyard in the UK.*

bear left beside a bench to return to the road and take B65 opposite, which descends to **Lower Adgestone Road**.

Entrance to Brading Butterfly Walk

View east from the top of Brading Down

> ⓘ *Bitterns successfully bred in Brading Marshes in 2018. These secretive birds are a type of heron, and the males make a distinctive far-carrying, booming sound in spring.*

4 Turn right and in 200m turn left up steps to take B48, soon with **Brading Roman Villa** on your right. Note that you do not need to pay the entrance fee to access the cafe and toilets. Continue along the driveway to another quiet road and turn left, then turn right and right again towards the **A3055**. Cross the road, turn left briefly, then turn right onto the **B3395**. Just over the railway bridge take B69 back towards **Brading station**.

To your right is the Eastern Yar river with Brading Marshes Nature Reserve on the other side of it. The nature reserve is the only RSPB nature reserve on the island and attracts a wide variety of birds year-round.

> ⓘ *The island was served by several railway lines until the 1960s. Nowadays the only National Railway line runs from Ryde to Shanklin.*

+ To lengthen

At Waypoint 2 the walk can be lengthened to incorporate a tour of the village centre. Turn right on the road to descend Brading's main street, turn left on Cross Street a little short of the church, bear right at the end, then just before the main road turn sharp left along a footpath to ascend to the main track along Nunwell Down. This adds about 1km (15min).

Brading Roman Villa

Brading Roman Villa

The villa dates from shortly after the Roman Conquest of the island in AD43 but was added to in stages over a few hundred years. The visitor centre and museum contain many Roman mosaics found at the site, Roman archaeology, as well as a permanent exhibition about the history of the site, including its excavation in the 1880s. A reconstructed Roman garden has also been built. Further information about the permanent exhibition as well as temporary exhibitions and events can be found at https://bradingromanvilla.org.uk.

Descending towards Shanklin Chine

WALK 3
Sandown and Shanklin

Start/finish	*Sandown Pier*
Locate	*///precluded.united.renting*
Cafes/pubs	*Many options on Sandown and Shanklin seafronts, some seasonal cafes on the clifftop part of the walk*
Transport	*Train to Sandown. Bus routes 2, 3 and 8*
Parking	*Sandown Esplanade (PO36 8LA)*
Toilets	*In Cliff Gardens, near Shanklin Chine, and on the sea wall*

Time 1hr 45min
Distance 7km (4.3 miles)
Climb 70m

An easy section of the Coastal Path between two popular resorts – cliffs on the way out, shoreline on the return

For anyone wanting a stroll by the sea, this route around Sandown Bay is a must. Very much a walk of two halves, it starts with an ascent from the seafront at Sandown, then takes a path – sometimes gently undulating – along the top of the sea cliffs, often with wonderful sea views, to the far side of Shanklin, descending to the shoreline via Shanklin Chine. Your return is initially along Shanklin seafront, then past beachfront chalets back towards Sandown.

Shanklin cliff lift

WALK 3 – SANDOWN AND SHANKLIN

Walking along Keats Green, Shanklin

1 Starting at **Sandown Pier** walk south along the esplanade, with the sea on your left. When the road ends, turn right up Ferncliff Path – bearing left up steps after a short distance – following the blue Coastal Path sign into Ferncliff Gardens. Stay on the main path through the gardens and soon emerge at the start of the clifftop path.

2 Remain on this level path, including where it becomes Cliff Road for a little while. There are far-reaching views of the sea and of the downland above Shanklin. In about 1.4km you are led along the far edge of Cliff Gardens onto the adjacent road where you turn left. Turn left again on footpath SS64 after just 80m, bringing you back to the cliff path.

3 Continue on the cliff path towards Shanklin. The concrete path undulates a bit more but is never taxing. Cross Hope Road 900m from the start of this section of the cliff path and continue uphill. Now overlooking Shanklin seafront, you soon pass a lift descending from clifftop to seashore. The lift was built in 1957 to replace a Victorian hydraulic lift that was destroyed during World War 2. A short distance after the lift is Keats Green, named after the 19th century poet John Keats, who frequently visited Shanklin. Beyond Keats Green start the descent to the

Entrance to Shanklin Chine

shoreline, passing the entrance to **Shanklin Chine** on the way.

The island's oldest tourist attraction, Shanklin Chine was opened in 1817. As well as its beautiful foliage, pretty trails and diverse bird and animal life – including resident chipmunks – the Chine boasts a 12m waterfall and romantic summer-night illuminations.

4 At the shoreline start walking along the seafront back towards Sandown. Where the seafront road

ⓘ *Picturesque Shanklin Old Village, the historic heart of Shanklin, features several eateries, gift shops and thatched cottages.*

bends left inland, continue past a car park and along a sea wall beside a row of brightly coloured chalets. Remain on this clockwise-curving path alongside **Hope Beach** and Welcome Beach, eventually returning to the pier at **Sandown**.

> **– To shorten**
> At Waypoint 3 the walk can be shortened by taking the footpath almost opposite descending to the shoreline. Once there turn left to return to Sandown. This option saves 3.4km (45min).

Sandown and Shanklin

Sandown and Shanklin are the most popular seaside resorts on the island, developed for tourism in the 19th century. As domestic tourism has declined, so have the resorts' fortunes, although Shanklin still possesses a lot of charm, with clean beaches, several independent shops, the quaint Old Village, and a generally pleasant atmosphere. Sandown seems to have suffered a little more but its beaches are well-used in summer, it boasts the only surviving pleasure pier, and the bay's seascape is enviable.

Shanklin Old Village

The church graveyard

WALK 4
Newchurch and the River Yar

Start/finish	*The Pointer Inn, Newchurch*
Locate	*///spurted.gambles.station*
Cafes/pubs	*Pub in Newchurch*
Transport	*Bus route 8 to Winford Cross (20min from start)*
Parking	*Newchurch car park, School Lane (PO36 0NL)*
Toilets	*No public toilets on route*

Time 1hr 15min
Distance 4.1km (2.5 miles)
Climb 50m

A pretty, rural walk in the centre of the island, well off the beaten track

This is a low-key but lovely walk. The first highlight is Newchurch Moors Nature Reserve, the largest nature reserve on the island: an attractive, verdant and tranquil place. After some woodland paths, your way descends to the broad and leafy Yar River Trail, once the Newport to Sandown railway line. A long section of this trail follows, before re-ascending back towards Newchurch.

Footpath descending to the Yar River Trail

Pointer Inn in Newchurch

1 From the **Pointer Inn**, follow footpath NC46 into the churchyard, noting the lovely garden below you. Bend right with the churchyard wall and just before the graveyard turn left down steps and right on the path below. When the graveyard ends and the wall turns right, turn right and walk along a broad path, now inside Newchurch Moors Nature Reserve.

Newchurch Moors Nature Reserve

WALK 4 – NEWCHURCH AND THE RIVER YAR

Newchurch Moors Nature Reserve is managed by the Hampshire and Isle of Wight Wildlife Trust, and even if you have little interest in the variety of visiting birdlife, its beauty and tranquillity make it a special place to linger.

2 In 90m turn left onto the first obvious path (soon passing benches), and at a path crossroads in 150m continue straight on. In a further 150m, bear half-right into the trees on an inconspicuous path. Turn right at the T-junction ahead and in 100m turn left into woodland, soon crossing a stream and ascending a rise to **Hill Farm** at the top.

3 Turn left through the farm and in 200m descend left into a beautiful wood. Ignore a left turn after 150m, and in a further 150m turn left at a T-junction. Ignore another left turn shortly afterwards and, in a further 150m, bear left back into the open and continue towards a gate visible below. Go through the gate to meet the broad

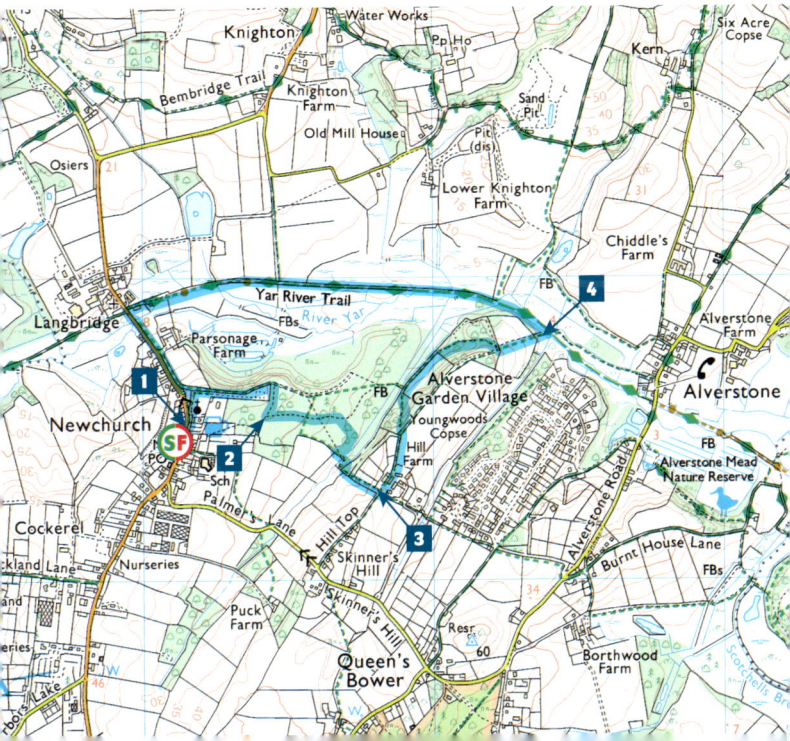

The Yar River Trail

track of the **Yar River Trail** and turn left along it. This section of the Yar River Trail follows the former railway line from Sandown to Newport, which ran from 1875 to 1956.

4 Stay on the Yar River Trail, running parallel to the **River Yar**, until you reach a road. Here, turn left onto a parallel footpath and walk up the hill

> ⓘ *There are many animal-related attractions on the island, not least the perennially popular (and free) Donkey Sanctuary near Wroxall.*

> ⓘ *The island is one of the few places in England still to have red squirrels. Grey squirrels are not permitted entry!*

towards the village centre. Just beyond a bend in the path, look out for steps on the right that ascend to the churchyard back in **Newchurch**. Continue in your current direction to retrace your steps back to the Pointer Inn.

WALK 5
Godshill and Freemantle Gate

Start/finish	The Griffin pub, Godshill
Locate	///offerings.composes.migrate
Cafes/pubs	Pub and tea rooms in Godshill
Transport	Bus routes 2 and 3
Parking	Car park opposite the Griffin pub (PO38 3JD)
Toilets	In car park opposite the pub

This short but sweet outing from Godshill heads initially up to the village church from where there are attractive views of the surrounding downland. After a short stretch on a quiet road, tracks ascend gradually to a potentially muddy footpath beside the boundary wall of the old Appuldurcombe Estate, and then Freemantle Gate. More attractive walking soon leads you into a wood and along a verdant footpath back to the pub. An optional detour takes you to Appuldurcombe House, once the grandest house on the island.

Time 1hr 30min
Distance 5.2km (3.2 miles)
Climb 130m

A rural circuit around picturesque Godshill with good views, a quiet wood, and the evocative Freemantle Gate

The Griffin pub, where the walk starts

Thatched cottages around Godshill church

1 Start at the Griffin pub in **Godshill**, opposite the village car park. Walk west along the main road through the village centre with its model village, quaint shops and tearooms. At the store/tourist information, turn left towards the **church** using either the narrow road or footpath (the latter was closed at time of writing). There is a nice view of the surrounding hills from the churchyard.

2 Retrace your steps to the road and continue along it in your current direction (don't go sharp right or left down Church Hollow). Remain on this minor road for 500m, ignoring a road joining from the left, then turn left onto **Sheepwash Lane**.

3 Look to your right on this road to spot St Catherine's Oratory Lighthouse and the Hoy Monument on St Catherine's Down in the distance (see Walk 8). After 400m on Sheepwash Lane, turn left onto

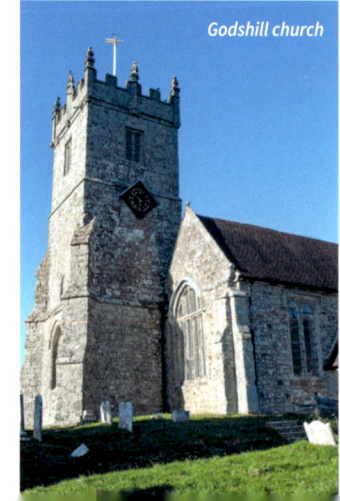

Godshill church

WALK 5 – GODSHILL AND FREEMANTLE GATE

bridleway GL56, climbing gradually to reach an obvious path junction beside **Stainham Farm**.

4 Ignore the descending path and continue your gradual ascent on GL58. In 450m ignore three adjacent field gates and continue on the main path through a different gate towards trees, a little more steeply this time. At a major junction in 300m take the left-most of the two paths going straight ahead, part of the Worsley Trail, which shortly runs beside the boundary wall of the former Appuldurcombe Estate. At the top of the initial rise is a

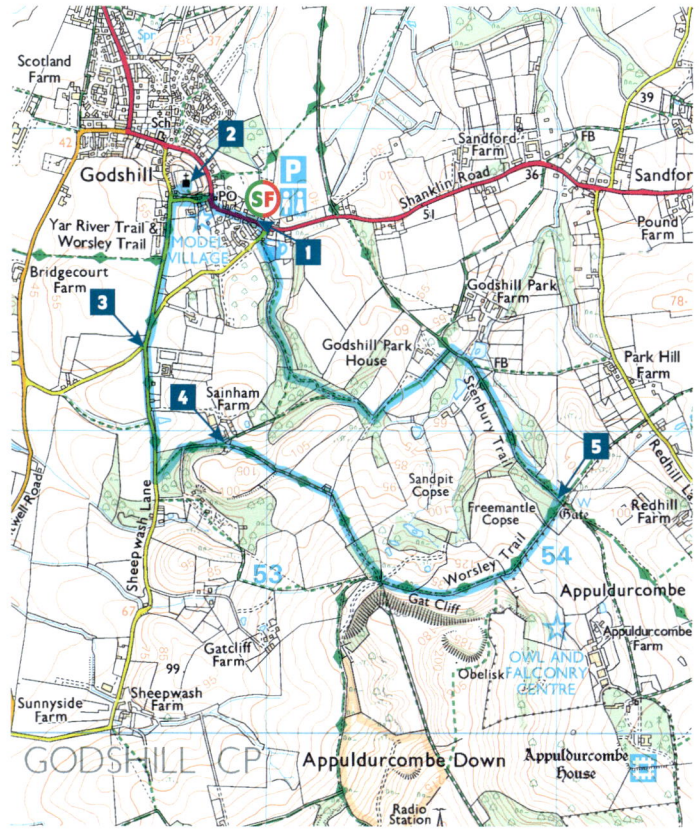

marvellous view towards the white cliffs of Culver Down. The path ends at a T-junction beside **Freemantle Gate**.

> Freemantle Gate is a very evocative and photogenic 18th-century neoclassical folly, built as an imposing entrance to the influential Worsley family's Appuldurcombe Estate. It was built primarily with Isle of Wight stone and is Grade 2 listed.

5 Turn left to descend a broad track and in 650m turn left onto GL56. At the end of the field go through a gate to enter woodland, and at a fork in 150m take the descending path right. Stay on the main path which descends to a T-junction beside a kissing gate. Go through the gate and follow the path to emerge alongside the garden at the rear of the Griffin pub. Turn right at the T-junction to return to the start of the walk.

> *ⓘ The 24km Worsley Trail runs across the southern part of the island, from Brighstone in the west to Shanklin in the east.*

Freemantle Gate

WALK 5 — GODSHILL AND FREEMANTLE GATE

View northeast towards Culver Down

✚ To lengthen

At Waypoint 5 walk through Freemantle Gate and continue on the main path to Appuldurcombe House. Now owned by English Heritage, the interior of the house is in ruins following a World War 2 bombing raid, but the exterior is beautiful, as are the grounds originally laid out by Capability Brown. This out-and-back detour will add about 20min to the walk.

Godshill

Pronounced 'godzill' by locals, the village consists of an attractive main street with numerous thatched buildings, souvenir shops and tearooms. It's a popular spot that can become crowded in summer. The 14th-century church is remarkable for its 15th-century 'Lily Cross' painting and is the second church to exist on the site. The first was built shortly before the Norman Conquest; as the church was being built, its foundations 'miraculously' made their way from a different spot to the current hilltop location. This was taken as a sign from God, hence the name Godshill.

The Winter Garden on Ventnor seafront

WALK 6
Ventnor and Bonchurch

Start/finish	Ventnor seafront
Locate	///logged.learn.soaps
Cafes/pubs	Several options in Ventnor
Transport	Bus routes 3 and 6
Parking	Eastern Esplanade car park (PO38 1EH)
Toilets	On Eastern Esplanade at start and at Monks Bay (100m off route)

Time 1hr
Distance 4.1km (2.5 miles)
Climb 60m

A long sea wall, Bonchurch Old Church and village centre with long pond, then quiet streets back to Ventnor

The first half of this walk follows a sea wall beneath cliffs, linking Ventnor to its much quieter neighbour Bonchurch. A path with hydrangeas and a lovely stream ascends gently to the village's original church dating from the 11th century. After a stroll through the charming main street with its beautiful pond, quiet residential roads and attractive clifftop paths are used to return to Ventnor.

Sea wall between Ventnor and Bonchurch

> ⓘ *Ventnor has its own micro-climate so is the perfect location for the island's botanic garden, on the western side of the resort.*

1 Start at the mosaic of Hygeia (goddess of health pictured on the town crest) at the eastern end of the small seafront at **Ventnor**. Head east to pass through the esplanade car park. Carry on along the sea wall past holiday homes and below cliffs. In 1.4km your way briefly becomes a private road. Just before a row of attractive waterfront houses turn inland up steps on a path passing above the houses, featuring beautiful hydrangeas and crossing bubbling Bonchurch Stream. For public toilets remain by the sea for a short while after the route turns inland. The path ends at Old St Boniface Church at **Bonchurch**. One of the oldest settlements on the island, Bonchurch was visited by many Victorian authors, including Charles Dickens, who stayed at nearby Winterbourne House.

2 Bear left to round the church, soon passing Winterbourne House. Bear left at the road junction ahead, staying in your current direction, to walk through the village centre. The long pond running beside the road is delightful and full of carp and other smaller fish. Continue along the road for 300m beyond the end of the pond, then turn left onto Madeira Road, initially running parallel to where you have just come from.

Old St Boniface Church, Bonchurch

Bonchurch village pond

3 Stay on this very pleasant road for 650m and bear left just after Kings Bay Road. At a T-junction with Wheelers Bay Road turn right then left onto Dudley Road. Immediately turn left again down Buono Vista Road and descend steps which lead to a lovely clifftop path. Where the path forks, stay on the path nearest the sea and start descending back to the seafront at Ventnor.

Ventnor

Ventnor seafront

Ventnor was little more than a fishing hamlet before the 19th century. The turning point came in 1829 when physician Sir James Clark extolled the virtues of the sunny and mild microclimate of the area. The next few decades saw great expansion: the railway arrived in 1866 (a branch line from Merstone followed in 1900), bringing in Victorian pleasure-seekers, and Churchill, Gandhi, Marx and Elgar all visited. The Botanic Garden, with around 30,000 species of rare and exotic plants and trees, is still a major attraction. The surrounding coastline is notoriously prone to landslip because of the vulnerable 'blue slipper' soft clay – a particularly bad landslip in 2023 caused much of the Coastal Path around here to be rerouted.

WALK 7
Niton Undercliff and St Catherine's Lighthouse

Time 1hr 45min
Distance 6.8km (4.2 miles)
Climb 175m

A short stretch of scenic Coastal Path, a fantastic descent to the Undercliff, then St Catherine's Lighthouse on the island's southern tip

Start/finish	St John the Baptist Church, Niton
Locate	///bypasses.glides.comply
Cafes/pubs	Pub and cafe in Niton, pub in Niton Undercliff (100m off route)
Transport	Bus route 6
Parking	On street, or small car park in Star Inn Road (PO38 2AZ)
Toilets	On Church Street, Niton

Under-visited Niton Undercliff has an almost Mediterranean ambience and feels separate from the rest of the island. This lovely walk starts high above the Undercliff, in Niton itself. After a short, steep climb to the sea cliffs, join the Coastal Path above a beautiful stretch of coastline before descending seabound on a verdant path. Descend further on delightful quiet lanes, skirt St Catherine's Lighthouse, then re-ascend gradually to Niton on more quiet lanes and paths.

Looking north towards the Knowles Farm Estate from the cliff-edge path

SHORT WALKS ISLE OF WIGHT

1 From the entrance to the **church** in Niton, head west on the road (against the flow of traffic). The stream you can see soon on your right is the fledgling Eastern Yar river (its source is just out of sight among bushes). Just after a left bend 300m from the start turn left up footpath NT33. The climb is quite steep but short. Continue over two stiles and along the left edge of a field. Turn right at a path T-junction just beyond the field, now on the **Coastal Path**.

Niton church

2 Continue along the Coastal Path on top of **West Cliff** for 650m, and just before a bench overlooking St Catherine's Lighthouse turn left down a lovely little footpath which becomes stepped and lushly verdant. At a lane at the bottom of the steps turn left, now in Niton Undercliff. At a T-junction in 400m turn right and then right again into another lane. At this junction detouring left instead of right will lead you in 100m to the Grade 2 listed Buddle Inn.

3 Remain on this lane as it descends obliquely towards the sea. In 450m take the gravel track to the right of a driveway to pass the National Trust-owned **Knowles Farm Estate**. Guglielmo Marconi conducted early wireless experiments behind the farmhouse in 1900. Continue past the holiday cottages on a broad grassy path and meander down to the sea at **Watershoot Bay**. The effects of erosion are all too clear here. Follow the coastline east on a path of sorts along the cliff edge towards the perimeter wall of **St Catherine's Lighthouse**.

Located on the island's most southerly point and commissioned after the notorious *Clarendon* shipwreck in 1836, St Catherine's Lighthouse came into operation in 1840. The new lighthouse was somewhat revolutionary in design and produced a powerful light by contemporary standards. It has been automated since 1997.

4 Walk around three sides of the lighthouse and, just before the path on the third side meets the cliff edge, bear left on a grassy path to resume following the coastline. Continue anticlockwise around the second and third

The approach to St Catherine's Lighthouse

The grassy clifftop path

sides of the field, then 100m from the start of the third side, bear right through a gap in the hedge and start ascending the next field. Go through a gate and emerge onto a lane at a bend.

5 Turn left to ascend the lane, soon regaining marvellous sea views. At a T-junction turn right, and at the next take the aptly named 'Tunnels' footpath opposite, continuing ahead at a junction. Turn right at the next junction (NT26). Come to a five-path junction after 500m and continue ahead (the second path clockwise). Ignore ways off and, on reaching a road, turn left and go across the crossroads to return to the church in **Niton**.

The Tunnels footpath

Niton Undercliff

Niton Undercliff is the island's most southerly village. Truly idyllic and under-explored (perhaps due to its relative inaccessibility), it developed into a proper community only in Victorian times, and it forms the western extremity of the wider Undercliff, which stretches to Ventnor. Its lush vegetation is testament to its warm microclimate. Guglielmo Marconi, the Italian pioneer of wireless communication, stayed and worked at the Royal Sandrock Hotel (near the Buddle Inn), which sadly burned down in the 1980s.

Gorse-covered cliffs

The Hoy Monument

WALK 8
St Catherine's Down

Start/finish	*Blackgang Viewpoint car park, near Blackgang Chine amusement park*
Locate	*///players.hacksaw.plantings*
Cafes/pubs	*None on route*
Transport	*Bus route 6 (ask to be let off at St Catherine's Down bus stop)*
Parking	*Car park at Blackgang Viewpoint (PO38 2JB)*
Toilets	*No public toilets on route*

Time 1hr 15min
Distance 4.6km (2.9 miles)
Climb 85m

An initial climb offers wonderful coastal views, followed by a medieval lighthouse and the secluded Hoy Monument

St Catherine's Oratory Lighthouse on top of St Catherine's Hill and the Hoy Monument on the other side of St Catherine's Down do not get the number of visitors they deserve, but this means that those who do visit are treated to a wonderful sense of near-solitude. After the walk, big and small children alike will appreciate an afternoon at Blackgang Chine, the UK's oldest amusement park (constructed in 1843).

Looking towards Blackgang Chine amusement park

Gorse on St Catherine's Down

1 From the car park cross the road and follow footpath C36 half-left, sign-posted to **Gore Down**. In 200m you meet a clear level path. Go left on it, now walking above Blackgang Chine amusement park visible on your left. Where the path peters out continue in your current direction. Soon there are fences on your left and right which converge at a stile: cross it and another to your right, keeping a fence on your right. From here there is a spectacular view of the 'Back of the Wight' coastline. Cross another stile after 200m and continue towards a gate visible in the centre of the narrow ridge, which is reached after 250m.

2 From the gate continue along the ridge of **St Catherine's Down**, enjoying the now-panoramic view. Wherever there's a fork take either option as long as you stay on top of the ridge. After 1km reach the **Hoy Monument** at the end of the ridge.

The 22m Hoy Monument was erected to commemorate a visit to England by Tsar Alexander I in 1814. Ironically, there is a plaque commemorating British losses (against Russian forces) in the Crimean War on the southern side.

3 Now turn around and head back along the ridge, maybe mixing up the paths where possible. Go back through the gate mentioned above, bear half-left and turn right at a fence to ascend **St Catherine's Hill** and reach St Catherine's Oratory Lighthouse.

WALK 8 – ST CATHERINE'S DOWN

51

St Catherine's Oratory Lighthouse

4 After admiring the sensational vista, bear half-right towards the sea. Beyond a gate, descend **Gore Down** on a wide grassy path towards the car park where you started the walk.

St Catherine's Oratory Lighthouse

St Catherine's Oratory Lighthouse (known as the 'Pepper Pot') – situated on one of the highest points on the island at 236m – was completed in 1328 by a landowner as punishment for stealing French wine. Solitary monks used to man the lighthouse until the adjoining oratory was demolished during the Dissolution of the Monasteries in the 16th century. Work began on a new lighthouse in 1785, but it was never competed so only the foundation stones are visible (below the radio mast nearby, and nicknamed the 'Salt Pot'). St Catherine's Lighthouse on the southern tip of the island was built instead (see Walk 7).

WALK 9
Afton Down and Compton Down

Start/finish	*Freshwater Bay*
Locate	*///troll.rocked.chickens*
Cafes/pubs	*Cafe and hotel bar/restaurant at Freshwater Bay*
Transport	*Bus route 12 and seasonal tourist services*
Parking	*Freshwater Bay long-stay car park (PO40 9TT)*
Toilets	*At Freshwater Bay*
Note	*The footpath up to the coastal road may be closed. Please check the council's footpath closure website (www.iow.gov.uk).*

Time 2hr 30min
Distance 10km (6.2 miles)
Climb 190m

A wonderful stretch of Coastal Path east of Freshwater Bay, then up onto the downs for the most dramatic part of the Tennyson Trail

This walk offers dramatic seascapes: towards the Needles and 'Back of the Wight' coastline initially, and towards the north coast near the end. There are many ascents, but the few that are steep are not long. From Freshwater Bay the cliff-hugging Coastal Path is followed to Compton Chine. A long inland section brings you to the stony Tennyson Trail along the ridge of Compton Down, and a descent through a spectacularly situated golf course provides a fitting climax. If the footpath up to the coastal road is closed, simply walk up the road from Freshwater Bay.

Freshwater Bay and Stag Rock

Mermaid Rock

1 Walk eastwards along the sea wall above the pebbled beach and, at its far side, go up some steps and turn right at the top, staying beside the sea. Bear right in 150m to walk along the cliff edge (although the left-hand option is also valid, and potentially safer). Stag Rock and Mermaid Rock can be seen here, broken off and cast adrift by violent weather. Soon pass a small Victorian monument and take the ascending path between road and sea, at the foot of **Afton Down**.

2 Continue along the stony path which eventually meets the road and runs alongside it. Shortly after a fence starts on your right, a footpath with a Coastal Path signpost leads you back towards the sea, the chalk cliffs now giving way to heavily eroded clay. Just before the path reaches **Compton Chine** turn left through a gate or over a stile, then right to cross the chine over a footbridge. Chine is a local word for a breach in the sea cliff.

> These cliffs contain rocks which are up to 126 million years old, and the National Trust beach below, at Compton Bay, is the best place on the island to spot dinosaur fossils at low tide.

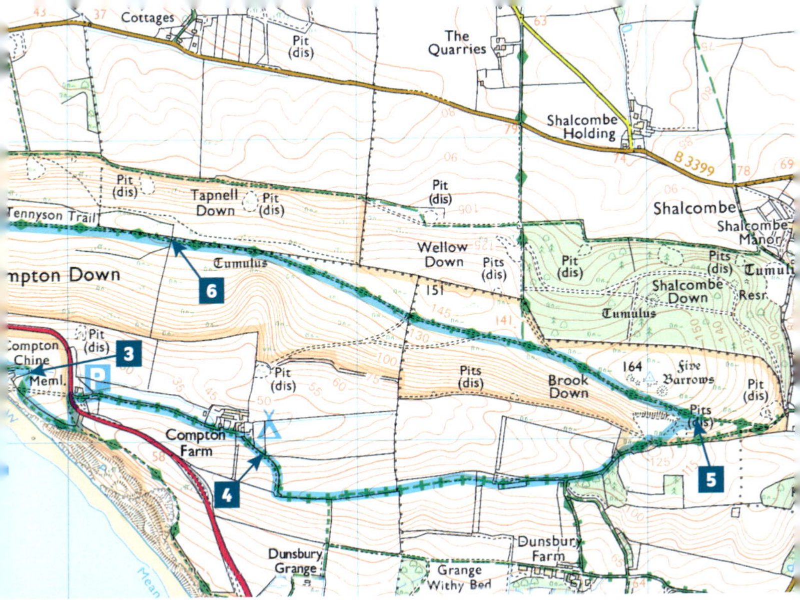

Victorian monument on the path

55

Compton Farm

3 Bear right and soon cross another stile to continue back on the clifftops. Descend briefly to a track and turn left through a gate, shortly turning right to cross the road and continue on byway F55. Continue towards and past **Compton Farm**.

> ⓘ *The chalk downs that run through the centre of the island contain over 200 'barrows', which are Neolithic communal burial mounds.*

4 Fork right 100m past the farm. The path soon levels out on top of a grassy ridge and in the distance you can see Brook Hill House. Built by the Seely family in 1901, the house was later leased by playwright JB Priestley, author of *An Inspector Calls*. At the end of this open ridge, ignore a descending footpath right to continue straight ahead on BS89 on a rough track. In 150m ignore a path forking right and ignore all other ways off your current direction until you are walking parallel to the ridge-top path up ahead. In 350m past the previous fork meet the broad, stony **Tennyson Trail**.

5 Turn left at this junction, going up the track towards the ridge you have just walked below.

For a short detour to Five Barrows, a Neolithic communal burial mound, go half-right to ascend the grassy escarpment, very steeply, heading towards the top of the Down. The panoramic view from up here is sensational. Descend westwards to rejoin the track.

Continue along the ridge in the direction of the chalk cliffs of Tennyson Down. When you enter **Freshwater**

> ⓘ *The 1970 Isle of Wight Festival featured The Doors, Jimi Hendrix and others; it was held on East Afton Down, to the north of the golf course.*

Bay Golf Course, 1.9km along the Tennyson Trail, a northerly view opens up to add to the drama.

6 Carry on through the golf course and in a further 1.5km bear left on a signposted footpath. On reaching the coastal road turn right along it to return to **Freshwater Bay**.

Freshwater Bay

The Needles, as seen from the viewpoint

WALK 10
Freshwater to Alum Bay

Time 2hr 15min
Distance 8.6km (5.3 miles)
Climb 245m

Start	Stroud Recreation Ground, School Green Road, Freshwater
Finish	Needles Landmark Attraction, Alum Bay
Locate	///cabinet.rejoins.loopholes
Cafes/pubs	Cafe and hotel bar/resturant at Freshwater Bay, tea room at Needles Old Battery, options at Needles Landmark Attraction
Transport	Bus routes 7 and 12 (to start and returning from finish) and seasonal tourist services
Parking	Moa Place long-stay car park (PO40 9AN)
Toilets	At Freshwater Bay

Pretty paths to Freshwater Bay then up and over the dramatic downs with two-coast views towards the Needles at the 'end of the island'

Definitely the most dramatic walk in this book! Attractive footpaths and quiet roads bring you to the sea at Freshwater Bay. Then you ascend to the Tennyson Monument, with spectacular views all the while, and go over the downs towards an incredible viewpoint overlooking the Needles. At the island's end, turn east and continue past the Needles Batteries towards the multi-coloured sands of Alum Bay.

Looking back towards Freshwater Bay and the 'Back of the Wight'

SHORT WALKS ISLE OF WIGHT

1 From the entrance to the Stroud Recreation Ground on School Green Road head east along the road to the Bow Bridge roundabout. Turn right down Stroud Road then in 80m bear left onto narrow footpath F37. When you meet a lane in 450m bear left, and at a road junction in a further 250m turn left downhill. In 100m turn right on F36. Eventually the path becomes a stony drive which leads you onto the coastal road at **Freshwater Bay**.

2 Cross the road. A brief detour towards the sea wall is worthwhile. Turn right and very shortly left (by toilets) following the blue **Coastal Path** arrow. After a short distance bear right, following another Coastal Path sign, to start the climb up **Tennyson Down**, taking the second left of four possible paths straight up the slope of the hill ahead and staying on the main broad path. Soon there's a comprehensive view back towards the 'Back of the Wight' coastline, and the north coast

WALK 10 – FRESHWATER TO ALUM BAY

also becomes visible. In about 600m spot the cross of the **Tennyson Monument** and head towards it.

The Tennyson Monument

The Tennyson Monument, with its granite cross, was erected in 1897 in memory of the famous Poet Laureate, who frequently left his home in Freshwater to walk on this down. *The Charge of the Light Brigade* is one work which was apparently written here.

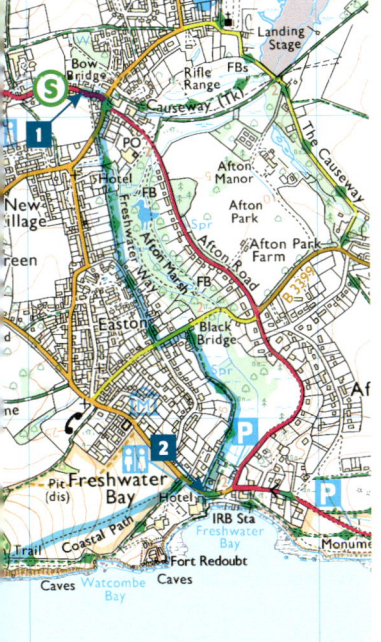

3 Beyond the monument head downhill along the ridge towards **West High Down** ahead. At a gate in 600m follow the Coastal Path signpost towards the Needles, bearing right at a fork in 150m. Continue along the path for 1.8km to another gate beside a transmitter; keep ahead initially but soon follow a stony path on the left of the ridge which descends to a concrete drive. Detour across the drive to take a short footpath to a **viewpoint** overlooking the Needles.

The Needles are three rock towers off the island's westernmost point. There were originally four 'needles', and ironically the only needle-like rock of the four was the one to collapse (in 1764). Wind speeds at the Needles are often the strongest in the UK.

4 Return to the drive and turn left to pass the coastguard station, then almost immediately (just before the entrance to the Needles New Battery) turn left up five steps and descend a concrete path. At the final corner before the **Needles Old Battery** look down for a magnificent view of **Scratchell's Bay**. Now follow the concrete drive (or a parallel stony path) which will eventually lead to the Needles Landmark Attraction at **Alum Bay**.

> ⓘ *The island was formed 8000–10,000 years ago, when the sea flooded the Solent valley at the end of the last ice age.*

The New Battery has a permanent exhibition illustrating its use as a site for missile and space rocket testing. The Old Battery saw action in both world wars but the bigger draw for tourists is the 'secret tunnel' leading to a fantastic view of the Needles. Both fortifications are owned by the National Trust.

Alum Bay and chairlift

Alum Bay has been a major attraction for as long as tourists have been visiting the island on account of its magnificent and uniquely multicoloured cliffs. The colouring is due to the presence of sulphates created by the oxidation of pyrite (ferrous sulphide). It is often said that there are 21 colours – although presumably what constitutes a colour is open to definition – and sand from the cliffs has been a traditional purchase ever since the early 19th century. A seasonal chairlift that has been in operation since 1971 transports visitors from the Needles Landmark Attraction down some 60m to the bay.

The multicoloured cliffs of Alum Bay

Footpath beside Widdick Chine towards the sea

WALK 11
Alum Bay to Colwell

Start	Needles Landmark Attraction, Alum Bay
Finish	Colwell
Locate	///crab.elsewhere.piled
Cafes/pubs	Options at Needles Landmark Attraction, restaurants and cafes in Totland Bay and Colwell Bay
Transport	Bus routes 7 and 12 and seasonal tourist services. Route 7 from walk's finish to return to Alum Bay
Parking	Car park at Needles Landmark Attraction (PO39 0JD)
Toilets	At Totland Bay and Colwell Bay

Time 1hr 15min
Distance 4.4km (2.7 miles)
Climb 70m

A moderate ascent up Headon Warren rewards with stunning views towards the Needles, then a long but beautiful stretch of sea wall

Autumn is the perfect season to enjoy this walk, when the heather on Headon Warren glows purple, contrasting with the blue sea and the green foliage of the heathland. Once Headon Warren is left, you descend back to the sea, then follow a broad sea wall around Totland Bay and Colwell Bay. There is a small selection of rather upmarket cafes and restaurants to choose from on this stretch.

View towards the Needles from Headon Warren

The purple heather of Headon Warren

1 From the attraction head east along the road. In 150m turn left along a drive, following a blue Coastal Path signpost. At a junction a short way ahead take the rightmost of three options, again following a Coastal Path sign. Ascend to a roughly circular open space, then take the wide grassy path on the right, now on **Headon Warren**, and almost immediately reach a fork.

2 Bear right at the fork and after a short distance swing left between gorse bushes. Look behind for a view of the Needles and soon there is another wonderful view towards the mainland. At a bench 200m beyond the last fork bear left. In a further 650m spot an information board and bench on your left then almost immediately turn left, following a Coastal Path arrow, leaving Headon Warren and taking a descending path above the sea to a road. Turn left and in 200m left again on a descending footpath beside **Widdick Chine** to the sea wall.

3 Turn right along the sea wall, now walking above the sandy beach of **Totland Bay**. Continue to reach **Totland Pier**.

Constructed in 1880, Totland Pier was closed 100 years later, as it was deemed unsafe. After decades of neglect, it was restored in 2019. However, further structural problems have caused the pier's closure again, and it is for sale at the time of writing.

SHORT WALKS ISLE OF WIGHT

Sandy beach at Totland Bay looking towards the pier

WALK 11 – ALUM BAY TO COLWELL

Colwell Bay

4 Remain on the sea wall beyond the pier. The fortress you can see on the mainland is Hurst Castle, and the island's Albert Fort can soon be seen as well. Totland Bay soon ends and the coloured chalets around **Colwell Bay** come into view. Just after the chalets end, turn right along Colwell Chine Road between two cafes and continue into **Colwell**. Bus stops for buses back to Alum Bay and to Yarmouth and Newport are to the left and right respectively at the end of this road.

Fort Albert and Hurst Castle

Fort Albert was a so-called Palmerston Fort, or Folly, one of many on the island and in the Solent in the 19th century, built to repel a potential French invasion. Prime Minister Lord Palmerston supported the Armed Forces' recommendation for their construction, but by the time they were constructed, the threat from the French Navy had largely disappeared! Hurst Castle was built 300 years earlier by King Henry VIII for exactly the same purpose (to repel the French). In the 17th century King Charles I was briefly imprisoned here on his final, fateful journey from Carisbrooke Castle to London. At just 1.3km, the distance between Fort Albert and Hurst Castle is the shortest distance between the mainland and island.

Going up the lane to Freshwater Old Village

WALK 12
Yarmouth and the Western Yar estuary

Time 1hr 45min
Distance 6.7km (4.2 miles)
Climb 40m

An easy and relaxing meander beside the river estuary, then quiet lanes, fields and woodland back to Yarmouth

Start/finish	Yarmouth bus stands/ferry terminal
Locate	///grinders.steam.mash
Cafes/pubs	Options in Yarmouth, pub at Freshwater Old Village
Transport	Ferry from Lymington. Bus route 7 and seasonal tourist services
Parking	Yarmouth long-stay car park (PO41 0NL)
Toilets	In ferry terminal

This walk is ideal for day-trippers catching the ferry from Lymington. It starts with a ramble on a 3km-long broad track beside the estuary of the Western Yar river. Then, after crossing the river on a delightful bridge, you ascend to Freshwater Old Village – perhaps getting a drink or bite to eat at the Red Lion – and return north along field and woodland footpaths, tracks and quiet lanes.

Stone bridge over the Western Yar

Wide footpath beside the Western Yar estuary

1 From the bus stands and visitor centre at Yarmouth, head west along the main road with the sea on your right. Just before the **swing bridge**, turn left down a concrete path beside Yarmouth sailing club to start your walk beside the Western Yar estuary.

The Western Yar river estuary has a huge array of resident and migrating birds. Many travel thousands of miles and rest here on their journey, replenishing their energy with the small sea creatures breeding on the mudflats. The saltmarshes developed after Yarmouth Harbour's breakwater was built in 1847, thus slowing down the flow of the river.

The path bends to the left and soon to the right to reach a tidal mill. Built in 1793 to replace a 17th-century wooden one, the tidal mill was once home to renowned 20th-century historian AJP Taylor.

2 From the mill, continue beside the estuary, ignoring ways off. At a lovely stone bridge 2.5km from the mill turn right onto the lane and continue up to **All Saints Church** (beside a pub) in Freshwater Old Village.

The tidal mill

WALK 12 – YARMOUTH AND THE WESTERN YAR ESTUARY

The church is of Saxon origin and contains several Tennyson memorials. Some members of his family – although not the poet himself – have been laid to rest in the churchyard.

3 Follow footpath F1 beside the church wall. Notice the amusing anecdote (and associated sculpture) about a drunk 19th-century smuggler. In 250m beyond the church continue in your current direction, now on

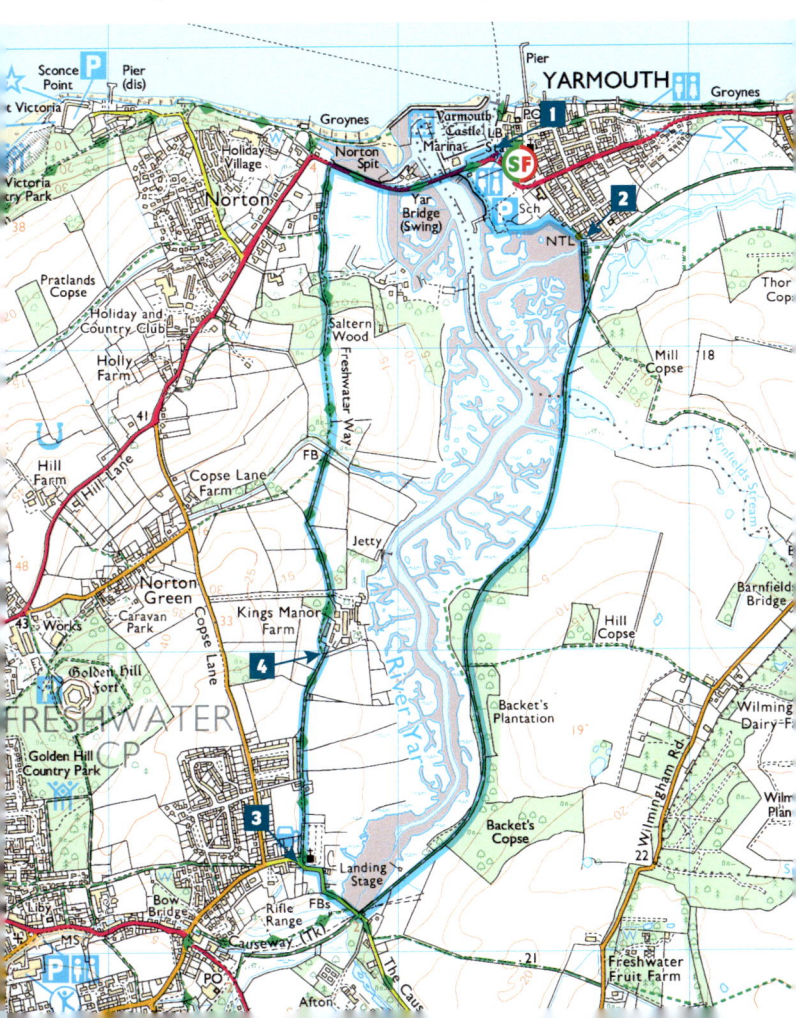

The graveyard at All Saints Church

a quiet lane, soon with a view down to the estuary, to just before **Kings Manor Farm**.

4 Take a parallel path on your left along the edge of a field, still following the Freshwater Way signposts as you pass through short stretches of woodland, alongside field edges and along tracks. Descend through **Saltern Wood** onto a broad track 1.2km from the farm and turn left along it. Soon come out onto the main road and turn right over the swing bridge to return to **Yarmouth**. In summer the bridge opens for ten minutes every hour or two to allow for vessels to pass.

Yarmouth

Yarmouth is one of the oldest towns on the island and one of the smallest in the UK. It has a special ambience: graceful and immediately appealing. The town's origins go back to Saxon times, and it was mentioned in the *Domesday Book* as 'Ermud' (muddy estuary), but the turning point came in 1135 when it received its charter. King John made the town his personal headquarters twice in the early 13th century and it managed to withstand 14th-century French raids (unlike nearby Newtown). However, as a precaution, Yarmouth Castle was constructed by Henry VIII, and is open to visitors (www.english-heritage.org.uk).

WALK 13
Newtown and Newtown Harbour

Start/finish	National Trust visitor centre at Newtown
Locate	///allies.types.songbirds
Cafes/pubs	Kiosk in car park
Transport	Bus route 7 to Hebberdens bus stop (20min from start)
Parking	Car park at Newtown visitor centre (PO30 4PA)
Toilets	In car park

Time 40min
Distance 2.4km (1.5 miles)
Climb 20m

This very short walk explores a village with a fascinating history, and a beautiful, unspoilt nature reserve

Peace and quiet are the watchwords as you explore the broad lanes of the village of Newtown – a bustling port in medieval times – and picturesque Newtown Harbour with its small boats and wide variety of birdlife. The quite unique 17th-century Old Town Hall might be open if renovations have been completed and provides the clearest indication of the sleepy village's fascinating past.

Coastguard Meadows

75

SHORT WALKS ISLE OF WIGHT

Wooden bridge in Newtown Harbour Nature Reserve

1 From the car park entrance, turn right past the Old Town Hall and descend the lane. On reaching a bridge spanning **Causeway Lake**, turn sharp right onto footpath CB16a, keeping the lake on your left. Beyond a gate in 80m keep beside the lake, enter a second field then ascend half-right towards the 19th-century Church of the Holy Spirit back in **Newtown**.

2 Continue ahead on the lane and bend left with it to its end. Continue on CB9 leading into Coastguard Meadows, then walk clockwise around two sides of the meadow and through a gap in the corner to start following a causeway through part of the **Newtown Harbour National Nature Reserve**. Soon bend right and – when facing a grassy path – left, aiming for a large hut. When you reach the hut, bend right and continue over a wooden bridge.

Newtown Harbour stands at the mouth of several streams and centuries ago it was the island's principal landing area, before silting led to its decline. Today it is a profoundly peaceful place. Winter is a great time to visit to see and hear migrating birds, such as Brent geese, teal and widgeon.

Bridge over Causeway Lake

The causeway in Newtown Harbour Nature Reserve

Bird hide in the nature reserve

> ⓘ *Actors Sheila Hancock and Jeremy Irons were born on the Isle of Wight.*

3 Beyond the bridge turn left to continue towards a bird hide. Carry on up a broad stony path which leads back to the lane you were on earlier. Turn left, passing the church again. Shortly afterwards look to your right to spot the old village pump, which was built around 1894. At the end of the lane turn right past the old village pub back towards the **Old Town Hall** and car park.

+ To lengthen
At the hut mentioned at Waypoint 2 you could turn left to detour on another causeway (muddy and uneven) to near the harbour mouth before returning to the hut to continue the walk. This adds 1.5km (around 30min).

Newtown

Newtown was originally known as Francheville ('Freetown') and was once the island's biggest and most prosperous settlement, due to its export of salt and oysters. However, a French raid in 1377, as well as the harbour clogging up with silt, reversed the town's fortunes and Newport soon overtook it in importance. The town was awarded two parliamentary seats in 1584, but the dwindling population and Great Reform Act of 1832 led to its disenfranchisement. Both John Churchill, first Duke of Marlborough, and Prime Minister George Canning served the constituency which, looking at the 'town' now, seems quite astonishing. The small and quirky 17th-century Old Town Hall contains exhibits of Newtown at its prime.

Old Town Hall, Newtown

St Mary's Church, Carisbrooke

WALK 14
Newport and Carisbrooke

Start/finish	*Newport bus station, South Street*
Locate	*///chaos.backs.cobbles*
Cafes/pubs	*In central Newport and Carisbrooke High Street*
Transport	*Bus routes 1, 2, 3, 5, 6, 7, 8, 9 and 12*
Parking	*Church Litten car park (PO30 1LL)*
Toilets	*At Post Office Lane, Newport, and Carisbrooke car park (100m off route)*

Time 1hr 30min
Distance 5.7km (3.5 miles)
Climb 75m

An attractive route from central Newport to Carisbrooke Castle, and an even nicer one back to Newport!

The walk starts with a brief saunter through central Newport – the island's small and relaxed capital – including the Minster and the high street, before taking quieter streets and then attractive footpaths beside woodland. Emerging at Carisbrooke church, more pleasant roads and footpaths lead to Carisbrooke Castle, where a visit is highly recommended. A long, lofty footpath leads back to Newport with views of the town and River Medina.

Pretty row of houses beside the ford across Lukely Brook

SHORT WALKS ISLE OF WIGHT

1 From the bus station, turn right on South Street and take the first road on the left (Town Lane). Continue past the Minster then turn left at the crossroads ahead, into High Street. The Minster on St Thomas' Square is Victorian, having replaced a 12th-century church. Cross the crossroads beside the Queen Victoria Memorial and after 100m turn right into Post Office Lane. At the end of the alleyway turn left, then first right and first left (Old Westminster Lane). Bear right at the first fork and right again by an old mill to join a concrete path leading into another quiet road. Continue in your current direction until you are beside **Victoria Recreation Ground**.

2 Continue on the shared-use concrete path ahead (footpath N58). Soon cross a road and carry on towards Carisbrooke. Turn left at a T-junction after 250m and, at a junction 100m

The entrance of Carisbrooke Castle

further on, turn left onto a new path which soon emerges in the churchyard of St Mary's Church in **Carisbrooke**.

3 Turn left just before the church, descend steps to the road, and take Castle Street almost opposite. At the end of this lovely little road continue ahead on a pretty footpath running beside a ford across **Lukely Brook**. Almost immediately after the end of this path, turn left onto Castle Lane and soon after turn right onto N192, ascending steps. Turn right at the top, and when the walls of **Carisbrooke Castle** come into view turn very sharply left on the stony track above the lane. To visit the castle, continue on the lane to reach the entrance.

4 Walk around two sides of the castle's outer walls and at the end of the second side turn left downhill, following a yellow arrow. Ignore a left fork to cross a road beside bus stops and take the steps opposite (N25). Beyond the steps the path rises gradually, soon with marvellous, ever-expanding

Ford across Lukely Brook

views beside Carisbrooke Cemetery on the top of **Mount Joy**.

5 The path descends to a suburban road; go left and take the first right (Elm Grove). Start walking anti-clockwise around the playing field ahead. By a metal post on its second side, descend the adjacent concrete path, ignore South View on the left and, at the T-junction beyond, turn right to reach another T-junction. Go right again past an architecturally splendid school building (built 1904), take the first left into Medina Avenue, then turn left again to walk through Church Litten Park. Founded in 1582, Church Litten Park was once a burial ground for the victims of plague, but was turned into a park in 1931. Newport bus station is at the other end of the small park.

The town was founded around 1180 by Richard de Redvers, then Lord of the Island, as a port settlement near Carisbrooke, and it was he who introduced the grid system of streets that still exists today. Its heyday was in Georgian times, following the decline in fortune of nearby Newtown and prior to the growth of Ryde and Cowes.

Carisbrooke Cemetery

WALK 14 – NEWPORT AND CARISBROOKE

Beautiful school building in Newport town centre

Carisbrooke Castle

Shortly after the Norman Invasion of 1066, the first Lord of the Island, William FitzOsbern, started work on Carisbrooke Castle, which was on the site of a Roman fort. After completion by his nephew Richard de Redvers, the castle was firstly an important fortification and secondly official residence of the island's lords and governors, until the last resident governor Princess Beatrice's death in 1944. Charles I was imprisoned here for over a year before his beheading in London in 1649. Maintained by English Heritage, the castle is hugely popular. Look out for the resident donkeys, which for centuries have drawn water from its well.

Looking towards Ryde Pier from the esplanade

WALK 15
Ryde to Fishbourne

Time 1hr 30min
Distance 5.4km (3.4 miles)
Climb 85m

Start	Ryde Esplanade station
Locate	///bound.claim.stray
Finish	Fishbourne
Cafes/pubs	Options at Ryde, tea garden at Quarr Abbey, pub at Fishbourne
Transport	Train to start. Bus routes 2, 3, 4, 8, 9. Bus 4 or 9 from walk's finish to return to Ryde
Parking	Car park in St Thomas Street, just west of pier (PO33 2DL)
Toilets	At Ryde Pier and Quarr Abbey

A quiet stroll along the Coastal Path through pretty Binstead leads to magnificent Quarr Abbey with its tea garden and pigs!

This is another family-friendly section of the Coastal Path. What it lacks in sea views it makes up for in tranquillity, birdsong and greenery. Quiet roads out of Ryde lead to a lovely footpath dissecting Ryde Golf Course, then up to Binstead – a village well off the beaten track. Beyond the ruins of a medieval abbey is the highlight of the walk: red-brick Quarr Abbey, a Benedictine monastery.

Gardens and tea garden at Quarr Abbey

SHORT WALKS ISLE OF WIGHT

> ⓘ *Ryde Pier is the oldest surviving pleasure pier in the world. At almost half a mile long, it is currently the UK's second-longest, after Southend Pier.*

1 From the station keep the sea on your right, walk past the small seaside green called Western Gardens, and continue into St Thomas Street. Take the first turning right (Buckingham Road) and bend left with the road to the top of the hill. Turn right here, now walking away from the town centre on this quiet residential street, with the occasional sea view on your right. At the end, pass between metal gates, then turn right onto a signed footpath parallel to the road ahead.

Thatched cottage in Binstead

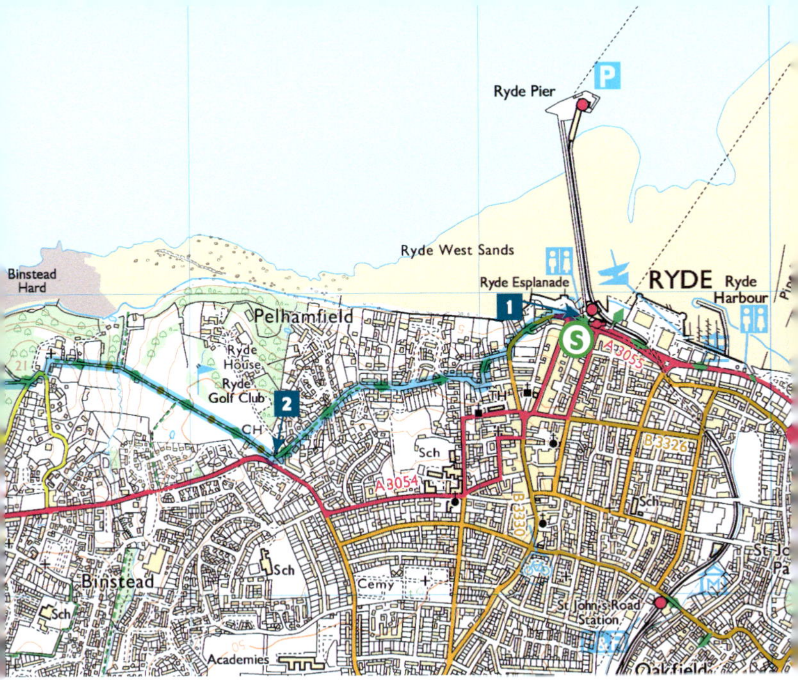

2 The footpath leads between the fairways of **Ryde Golf Course**. Cross a brook at the bottom of the hill and continue on this lovely path. At the top of the next ascent is the village of **Binstead**. Continue past the church, turn right at the junction almost immediately after it, and right again on a signposted driveway 30m later. The paving ends at a house and becomes a gravel track. Turn right when this track ends and in 500m pass the ruins of the pre-Reformation **Old Quarr Abbey**.

Pig enclosure at Quarr Abbey

The ruins of Old Quarr Abbey

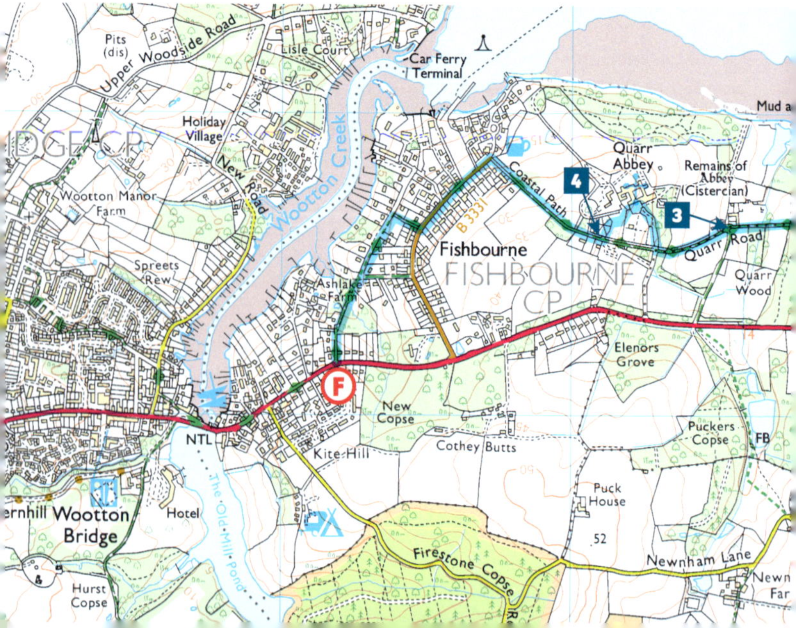

> Old Quarr Abbey was constructed from 1132 and demolished in 1536 during the Dissolution of the Monasteries under Henry VIII. It was the foremost religious institution on the island.

3 In a further 350m reach the driveway of the current **Quarr Abbey**. Turn right here towards the abbey. The red-brick abbey buildings are passed first, followed by the tea garden on the left, and shop and visitor centre on the right. Shortly bear right off the main path to pass the resident pigs, kept as part of monastic tradition.

4 Turn right on the track beyond (the one you were on before the abbey) and descend to meet the road running through **Fishbourne**, opposite a pub. Turn left. The ferry terminal for Portsmouth is a little way along. In 250m look out for an easy-to-miss signed footpath on your right and follow this to a T-junction. Turn left and in 200m continue ahead on a path, following the Coastal Path sign. This continues to the main road (**A3054**) beside the stop for the bus back to Ryde.

> **+ To lengthen**
> From the end of the walk, you could continue down the A3054 for 10min (600m) to Wootton Bridge (the name of the area as well as the attractive bridge spanning Wootton Creek), where there is a pub and other refreshment options.

Quarr Abbey

Quarr Abbey

The present Quarr Abbey (pronounced 'cor') is named after an important nearby quarry mined since Roman times, which provided materials to build Winchester and Chichester cathedrals, and Winchester College. It was completed in 1912 to house a French Benedictine order, persecuted in France. Many of the original monks returned to France in 1922 and English monks moved in, but it took a further 15 years for the abbey to become independent of France. It is today still actively used and maintained by about ten Benedictine followers. Admission to the visitor centre, the grounds and the abbey church is free, though donations are welcome. Check out the very comprehensive website (www.quarrabbey.org).

Yarmouth pier (Walk 12)

USEFUL INFORMATION

Footpath closures

Footpaths closures are not uncommon, especially in coastal areas due to the unpredictable effects of erosion and landslips. Before setting out on any walk, consult the Council's footpath closures webpage via their website www.iow.gov.uk (search for 'path closures').

Tourist information

For up-to-date information including current events, accommodation and where to eat www.visitisleofwight.co.uk

There are 12 Tourist Information Points across the island, in Bembridge, Brighstone, East Cowes, Freshwater Bay, Godshill, Havenstreet, Newport, Ryde, Sandown, Shanklin, Ventnor and Yarmouth.

For more detailed information, look at the weekly Isle of Wight County Press www.iwcp.co.uk

Transport

Ferries
Wightlink www.wightlink.co.uk

Red Funnel www.redfunnel.co.uk

Hovercraft
Hovertravel www.hovertravel.co.uk

The following car-ferry services can also be used by foot passengers:

MAINLAND	ISLAND	JOURNEY TIME	OPERATOR
Portsmouth Harbour	Fishbourne (near Ryde)	40min	Wightlink
Southampton Town Quay	East Cowes	1hr	Red Funnel
Lymington Pier	Yarmouth	35min	Wightlink

The following services are for foot passengers only:

MAINLAND	ISLAND	JOURNEY TIME	SEACRAFT	OPERATOR
Portsmouth Harbour Station	Ryde Pier	20min	Catamaran	Wightlink
Southsea (Clarence Pier)	Ryde Esplanade	10min	Hovercraft	Hovertravel
Southampton Town Quay	(West) Cowes	25min	Catamaran	Red Funnel

Buses
Southern Vectis www.islandbuses.info

Train
Island Line www.southwesternrailway.com

Parking

For car park locations and charges go to www.iwight.com and search for 'parking'

Tide times

www.isleofwight.com/tide-times

© Paul Curtis 2026
First edition 2026
ISBN: 978 1 78631 255 6
eISBN: 978 1 78765 234 7

Printed in China on responsibly sourced paper on behalf of Latitude Press Ltd
A catalogue record for this book is available from the British Library.
All photographs are by the author unless otherwise stated.
Cover illustration of the Needles by Clare Crooke.

© Crown copyright and database rights 2026 OS AC0000810376

Cicerone's EU representative for GPSR compliance is Easy Access System Europe, Mustamäe tee 50, 10621 Tallinn, Estonia. Email gpsr.requests@easproject.com.

CICERONE

Cicerone Press, Juniper House, Murley Moss, Oxenholme Road,
Kendal, Cumbria, LA9 7RL

www.cicerone.co.uk

Updates to this Guide

While every effort is made to ensure the accuracy of guidebooks as they go to print, changes can occur during the lifetime of an edition. Any updates that we know of for this guide will be on the Cicerone website (www.cicerone.co.uk/1255/updates), so please check before planning your trip. We also advise that you check information about transport, accommodation and shops locally. Even rights of way can be altered over time. We are always grateful for information about any discrepancies between a guidebook and the facts on the ground, sent by email to updates@cicerone.co.uk.

Register your book: To sign up to receive free updates, special offers and GPX files where available, create a Cicerone account and register your purchase via the 'My Account' tab at www.cicerone.co.uk.